GREECE
the people

Sierra Adare

A Bobbie Kalman Book

The Lands, Peoples, and Cultures Series

 Crabtree Publishing Company
www.crabtreebooks.com

The Lands, Peoples, and Cultures Series
Created by Bobbie Kalman

Editors
Virginia Mainprize
Ellen Rodger
Proofreader: Adrianna Morganelli

Computer technology advisor
Robert MacGregor

Project development, writing, and design
Water Buffalo Books
Mark Sachner — editor
Sabine Baupré — design
MaryLee Knowlton
Joyce Funamoto

Revisions and Updates
Plan B Book Packagers
Redbud Editorial

Ilustrations
George Balbar

Special thanks to:
The Greek Tourism Office and Office of the Minister of Business, New York; Gonda Van Steen, Department of Classics, University of Arizona; the Panos family; Marsha Baddeley

Photographs
Susan Alworth: p. 5 (top), p.11 (bottom), p.13 (bottom); Andrey Grinyov/Shutterstock, Inc.: p. 1; Jessica L Archibald/Shutterstock, Inc.: p. 23 (top); Artifan/Shutterstock, Inc.: p. 13 (top); Bill Bachmann/Bruce Coleman, Inc.: cover; Marc Crabtree: p. 21 (bottom), p. 24; Farrell Grehan/Photo Researchers: p. 17 (top); Elpis Ioannidis/Shutterstock, Inc.: p. 28; Mike Jackson/Photo Researchers: p. 11 (top); janprchal/Shutterstock, Inc.: p. 9 (bottom right); Wolfgang Kaehler: p. 3, p. 4, p. 15 (top), p. 16, p. 21 (top), p. 23 (bottom), p. 27; rj lerich/Shutterstock, Inc.: p. 8, p. 10, p. 12; Ingrid Marn: p. 22; Timothy R. Nichols/Shutterstock, Inc.: p. 9 (bottom left), 29 (top); Ninatallah/Art Resource, NY: p. 6; L T O'Reilly/Shutterstock, Inc.: p. 18; Pierdelune/Shutterstock, Inc.: p. 25 (top); Carl Purcell: p. 5 (left), p. 17 (bottom), p. 19, p. 30; Michael Ransburg/Shutterstock, Inc.: p. 26 (bottom); David H. Seymour/Shutterstock, Inc.: p. 7; Scala/Art Resource, NY: p. 9; Ljupco Smokovski/Shutterstock, Inc.: p. 29 (top); Michael Stokes/Shutterstock, Inc.: p. 20; Zdorov Kirill Vladimirovich/Shutterstock, Inc.: p. 14, p. 25 (bottom), p. 26 (top); WizData, inc./Shutterstock, Inc.: p. 31

Every effort has been made to obtain the appropriate credit and full copyright clearance for all images in this book. Any oversites, despite Crabtree's greatest precautions, will be corrected in future editions.

Cover
Many volunteers dressed up in traditional Greek costumes to welcome tourists from around the world to the 2004 summer Olympics in Greece, birthplace of the very first Olympic games.

Title page
Boats are moored in a harbor on the island of Santorini.

Library and Archives Canada Cataloguing in Publication

Adare, Sierra
    Greece : the people / Sierra Adare.

(Lands, peoples, and cultures series)
Includes index.
ISBN 978-0-7787-9309-0 (bound).--ISBN 978-0-7787-9677-0 (pbk.)

    1. Greece--Social conditions--1974- --Juvenile literature.
I. Title. II. Series.

HN650.5.A8A32 2007   j949.5   C2007-906217-2

Library of Congress Cataloging-in-Publication Data

Adare, Sierra.
    Greece. the people / Sierra Adare. -- [Rev. ed.].
        p. cm. -- (Lands, peoples, and cultures)
    Includes index.
    ISBN-13: 978-0-7787-9309-0 (rlb)
    ISBN-10: 0-7787-9309-5 (rlb)
    ISBN-13: 978-0-7787-9677-0 (pb)
    ISBN-10: 0-7787-9677-9 (pb)
    1. Greece--Social life and customs--Juvenile literature. I. Title. II. Series.

DF741.A33 2007
949.5--dc22
                                                          2007041637

Crabtree Publishing Company
www.crabtreebooks.com   1-800-387-7650

Published in Canada
Crabtree Publishing
616 Welland Ave.
St. Catharines, ON
L2M 5V6

Published in the United States
Crabtree Publishing
PMB16A
350 Fifth Ave., Suite 3308
New York, NY 10118

Published in the United Kingdom
Crabtree Publishing
White Cross Mills
High Town, Lancaster
LA1 4XS

Published in Australia
Crabtree Publishing
386 Mt. Alexander Rd.
Ascot Vale (Melbourne)
VIC 3032

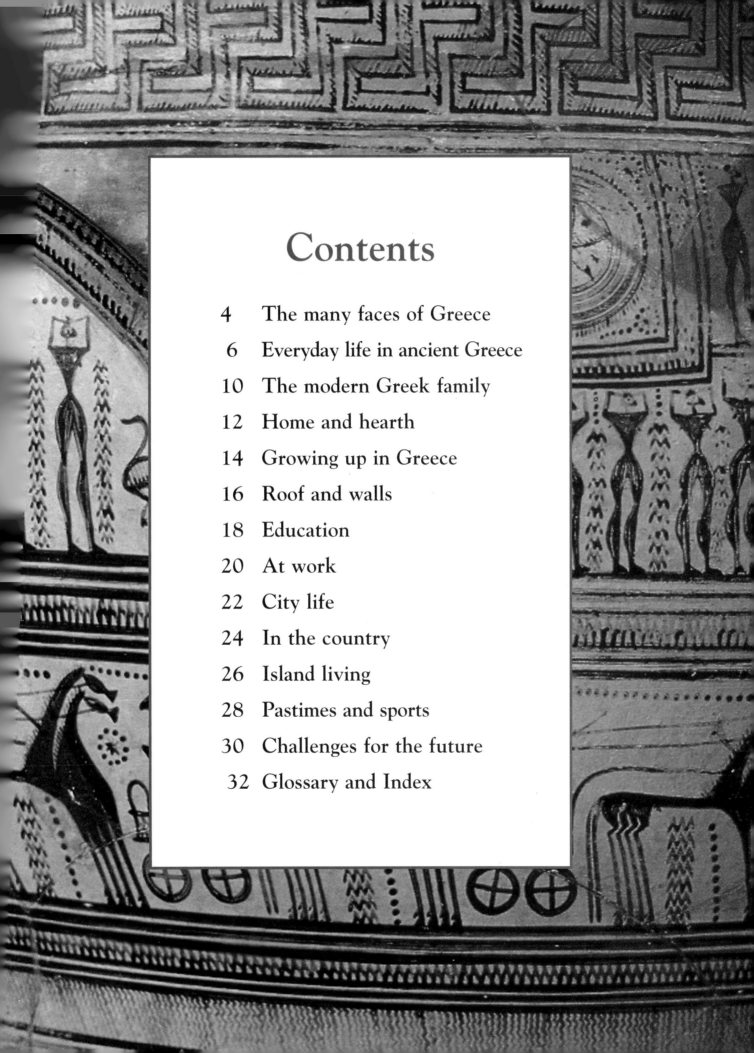

Contents

Thousands of years ago, many groups of people from Europe, Africa, and central Asia settled in Greece. Some of these groups moved on to other regions. Some stayed and were conquered by more powerful **civilizations**. These people are the ancestors of the Greeks.

What is an ethnic Greek?

Today, 98 percent of the people living in Greece are ethnic Greeks. They are descended from the ancient Greeks and the many non-Greek peoples who lived in Greece in ancient times. These groups of people have included the Persians, Macedonians, Romans, and Turks. Modern Greeks share a common language and practice the **Greek Orthodox** religion. These factors make Greece one of the most **homogeneous** nations in Europe.

Greeks abroad

Greeks are travelers and have settled in many countries. For centuries, there have been thriving Greek communities in Istanbul, Turkey, and Alexandria, the commercial capital of Egypt. Greek **immigrants** have brought their rich culture and traditions to their homes in North America, Australia, and other parts of Europe. Wherever they are, Greeks cherish the memory of their homeland and dream of returning one day, even if only for a visit.

Almost eleven million people live in Greece today.

Turkish Greeks

About five percent of Greeks are of non-Greek origin. They come from several ethnic and religious backgrounds. About 100,000 people of Turkish descent live in Greece. Turkish-Greeks are citizens of Greece. They speak the Turkish language and follow the teachings of Islam, the Muslim religion. Many Turkish-Greek women wear long black overcoats and white scarves, called *yashmaks*, that cover their heads and shoulders.

Some of these Turkish Greeks live in Thrace, the province that borders Turkey in northeastern Greece. Others live on the Dodecanese Islands, which lie just off the Turkish coast. These islands were part of Turkey until 1947.

(top) Two older men share a drink at a café.

(below) A young man in ceremonial costume stands guard at a war memorial.

Jewish heritage

Greece has a Jewish community that dates back over 2,000 years. In the late 1400s, many Jews left Spain because they were being **persecuted** for their religious beliefs. They settled in Greece, where they were allowed to practice their religion freely. The Jewish population of Greece grew to about 70,000. During **World War II**, Germany invaded Greece. The **Nazis** sent thousands of Jews and Greeks who resisted them to concentration camps, where they were murdered. The Jewish community was reduced to 5,000 people.

Roma

Greece has a large population of Roma people. The Roma speak an ancient language, called Romany. Some Roma are nomadic. They travel throughout the country selling goods and horses, and they live in trailers. Other Romas have settled permanently in towns. The Roma people sometimes suffer from **descrimination** in employment, housing, and education.

The ancient Greeks established **city-states** around 800 B.C. The city-state was an independent city that controlled surrounding towns and farming areas, much like a country. The Greek city-states of Athens, Sparta, Corinth, and Thebes, had their own governments and armies. City-states often went to war with each other to control trade and territory.

The agora

The agora, or marketplace, was the center of everyday life in most city-states. It was a large open space in the middle of the town, surrounded by public buildings, offices, and shops. Early each morning, the agora began to fill with people. Merchants opened their shops, and villagers set up stalls, selling vegetables, wine, cheese, and live sheep and goats. The agora was a noisy, busy place.

Men came to do the daily shopping, often with the help of a slave, who carried the groceries home. Few homes had their own well, so women came to collect water at the public well in the agora.

A workday

In ancient Greece, the workday began at dawn. Men in Athens had many jobs. Some worked in government, some were potters who made and sold clay pots and urns, and some made jewelry or shoes. Others were blacksmiths who made plows and weapons. The ancient Greeks preferred to run their own businesses and be their own bosses. Some men hired themselves out as day laborers on farms and in vineyards.

(right) The Ancient Greeks worshiped many different gods at temples. This one is dedicated to Poseidon, god of the sea.

Inside an ancient temple

The people of Athens built the Parthenon between 447 and 432 B.C. It was a temple dedicated to Athena Parthenos, Athena the Maiden, the patron goddess of their city. The temple was a marvel of marble. Even the roof was made of marble tiles about one inch (2.5 cm) thick. Statues adorned the Parthenon both inside and out. In the *naos*, the inner room, stood a 40-foot (12-meter) gold and ivory statue of Athena holding her shield. To this day, the Parthenon sits on top of the Acropolis, the once-fortified hilltop in the center of Athens.

This is a copy of the statue of Athena. The original disappeared long ago.

The Acropolis in Athens is located on a hill overlooking the city. It was a fortress and a place where Athenians held ceremonies. Several other temples are located nearby.

Strong women of Sparta

In contrast to women in other city-states, women and girls in Sparta had more freedom. Sparta was a warrior society where every free man was a soldier, and military discipline and physical training were very important. Women were encouraged to exercise so they could give birth to strong boys. At times in Sparta's history, women were allowed to meet with men outside their homes and could even own property. Like all other women in ancient Greece, they were not allowed to vote.

Sweating and bathing

The ancient Greeks believed in the importance of a healthy body. At the end of the workday, men stopped off at the gymnasium for a workout and a bath. At sunset, they returned home for dinner. Men ate separately from women and often entertained other men in the evening. In wealthy households, slaves served the food, and musicians and dancing girls entertained the guests.

Women stay at home

Ancient Greek women had few rights. They could not vote in elections and were expected to obey their husbands. They spent most of their time at home, managing their slaves, if they were wealthy, or doing the housework themselves. Public spaces, such as the agora, were mainly for men. Women stayed home and looked after home and the children.

Boys and girls

When they were six, boys in the ancient city-state of Athens were sent to school, where they learned to read and write. Instead of using a pencil and paper, they wrote on wax tablets with a stylus, a tool with a sharp end to cut into the wax and a soft end to rub out mistakes. With the help of an abacus, a calculator with counter beads that slide along rods, students studied arithmetic. Boys also took music lessons, learning to play the lyre, a small instrument that looks and sounds like the harp.

Boys stayed in school until they were fifteen. At eighteen, they became citizens of Athens and joined the army for one or two years. They could then take up a trade, work for the government, or if they came from a wealthy family, enter a sports academy.

Girls did not go to school. They stayed home with their mothers, who taught them to spin, weave, and cook. When they were about fifteen, girls married men who were usually twice their age. Fathers chose their daughters' husband', and the brides did not meet the grooms until their wedding days.

(above) At a time when women were taught only the basics of reading and writing, Sappho was an exception. She ran a school for girls on the island of Lesbos where they were taught music, singing, poetry, and writing. Sappho wrote nine books of poetry, and the Greek philosopher Plato considered her one of the greatest poets of the ancient world.

(below left) An ancient agora temple in Athens.

(below) An ancient Greek warrior, or **hoplite,** *wore a helmet like this one.*

9

The modern Greek family

Family life is very important to Greeks. Greek families maintain many traditions, especially in the villages. Mothers have a special position of honor. People tend to live close to their extended family, their grandparents, aunts, uncles, and cousins. Relatives give help and advice to each other. Older people are respected and often live with and are cared for by their children and grandchildren.

Parents and children

Although parents are very loving toward their children, they often raise them quite strictly. Children are expected to show respect to their elders. In their spare time, children are also expected to help on the farm or in the family business. Holidays and anniversaries are family events that everyone attends.

The dowry tradition

Many years ago, Greek families chose their children's marriage partners. Arranged marriages are now illegal. Today, young people decide whom they want to marry. Another old marriage tradition involved paying a dowry when a daughter marries. A dowry is money or property a woman brings to her husband when she gets married. Greek law limits the size of the dowry, forbidding any that will **impoverish** the bride's family.

It is still a custom in rural areas of Greece, for families to give their daughter a house and furniture when she gets married. Some parents may give her their house and move to a smaller house or apartment. Others may rent an apartment in the same building.

A fisherman cleans octopi by the sea. Octopus is a delicacy often served fried or marinated in olive oil, and eaten at family gatherings and meals.

(above) Family and friends enjoy a meal together at a seaside restaurant in the Cyclades Islands.

Sometimes, parents add another level onto their house for the young couple. Instead of a traditional dowry, some girls are sent to university in Greece or another country.

Too close for comfort?

In northern regions, the groom often brings his bride to live with his family. Moving in with her husband's parents can be a difficult adjustment for a young woman. Especially until she has children of her own, she may find she is bossed around by her mother-in-law. In some families, three generations live together. Grandparents often help look after children, allowing both parents to work outside the home.

(right) A Greek grandmother cares for her grandchild while the child's parents work.

Women in the city-states of ancient Greece stayed at home. They rarely appeared in public except at festivals and funerals. Usually with the help of slaves, women looked after the household chores, such as preparing meals, cleaning, and caring for the children. Women did not eat with their husbands. They lived in a separate area of the house, which was not so well decorated as the men's section.

A modern washing machine sits outside a traditional Greek island home.

Women today

Many Greek women are still tied to the home. Women make up most of university graduates in the country but most Greek women marry in their twenties and begin having children. Even if she has a job, a married woman is responsible for cooking and cleaning, shopping, doing the laundry, and looking after the children. Men do chores outside the home. In some families, especially in rural villages, fathers, sons, and male guests eat separately from the women. Greek cafés are often filled with men, drinking coffee or sipping *ouzo*, a strong alcoholic drink. The women are at home preparing dinner or finishing the housework.

The changing role of women

In the early 1980s, the **feminist movement** began to affect Greek society. Women have jobs outside the home, but men, on the whole, are better paid. Greek women take home about three quarters of what men do for the same job. Most women work in lower-paying jobs, such as clerks, secretaries, and factory workers. Some are entering professions that until recently were controlled by men.

(top) The ancient Greeks considered law courts to be important institutions. Today, more Greek women are becoming lawyers.

Childcare and nannies

Today, many Greek women work outside of the home, and fewer couples move in with their parents. Some young families hire **nannies** to live in the home and help care for the children. Especially in the cities, many parents want their children to have a **foreign** nanny. English- and German-speaking women are in great demand because they can teach the children the language and customs of another culture. The government funds some childcare, but not nearly enough to meet the need. Most families still rely on private daycare, nannies, and grandparents to provide care for young children while parents work.

In the cities and villages, many women run family-owned shops and restaurants.

Greek families, especially in the cities, are smaller today than they were in the past. Parents usually have only two children. Since many families live in the same village, house, or apartment building, relatives stay in constant contact with each other. Cousins play together and are as close as brothers and sisters. Children also grow up as part of a *paréa*, a group of tightly knit friends who usually go through life together. When a young woman marries, she may bring her new husband into her *paréa* and join his *paréa* as well.

Most Greek children are baptized in churches like this one on the island of Crete.

What's in a name?
According to tradition, Greek parents name their first son after his grandfather on his father's side. On mainland Greece, the first daughter gets her father's mother's name. In the Aegean Islands, the first girl is traditionally named after her grandmother on her mother's side. Today, this custom may apply to one of the girl's middle names only, while her first name comes from a popular soap opera or television show! In the Greek Orthodox religious tradition, girls have one first name and two middle names.

Nameday parties

Greek children celebrate both their birthdays and their namedays. In the Greek Orthodox community, every day is dedicated to a saint. On May 21, St. Helen's Day, for example, every girl named Helen celebrates her nameday. Her parents throw a party with food and sweets. Family and friends stop by with their good wishes, a card, or a gift.

Just for fun

In Greece, children do many of the same things for fun that kids do in other parts of the world. Kids play ball in the town square, skateboard in the streets, or play computer games with their friends. When the weather is nice, families go to visit relatives in the country or on another island. Parents or grandparents take the kids to the movies, the theater, or maybe the museum. They go out for ice cream, too.

(right) A woman relaxing with her children at home on an island in the Aegean Sea.

(below) A father and son out for a walk pass by posters on a street in Athens.

15

Greece is a land of contrasts: crowded cities and small farms, isolated island villages and sprawling mainland suburbs. The types of houses Greeks live in depend on the land, the climate, and the economic and cultural background of the people who own them.

Village houses

In villages, farmhouses are usually clustered closely together and are surrounded by fields and farmland. The flat-roofed houses are small, with three or four rooms, wood or earth floors, and a small kitchen. Many of these houses are simply furnished, with a few wooden chairs, a table, and low beds. In warmer regions, part of the kitchen may be outside the house, and most of the cooking is done in the open air. Families spend a lot of time outdoors. A small garden, a porch or balcony, or a courtyard are favorite places to eat meals, chat with friends, or just relax after a busy day.

Island and mountain living

In the mountains of the north, many homes have two or three stories and pointed roofs to keep the snow from piling up. The first floor is often a cellar or workshop. The second floor provides warm winter quarters for the family.

House styles on the islands are quite different, and they change from region to region. On Crete, far off in the southern Mediterranean, where the temperature gets very hot in the summer, the houses are wide and low to deflect the sunlight.

On the Cyclades Islands, gleaming villages of flat-roofed houses cling to the hillsides. Large cisterns collect rainwater off the roof. The winding lanes between the houses are often too narrow for cars. Motorcycles and the occasional donkey, laden with supplies or firewood, are the only way of getting around the village.

The rooftop terrace on this house is perfectly suited to the warm, sunny climate of Santorini, a Cyclades Island in the southern Aegean Sea.

Ancient homes

Houses in ancient Greece were built of mud bricks on a stone foundation. Since the bricks were not baked, they were soft and easy for burglars to break through. Houses were built around a courtyard. Rooms looked onto the courtyard and not out on the noisy, smelly street. The family lived in the back of the house. The women's quarters were upstairs.

City homes

In towns and cities, where there is a shortage of housing, most people are crowded into apartment blocks that stretch as far as the eye can see. In the suburbs of Athens and other cities, wealthier families may have their own home. Usually, it is a two-story building of concrete and brick, painted white or bright colors. Because their homes are often small, Greeks meet their friends for a coffee or a meal at the local café or taverna.

(above) A stone farmhouse has a clay roof.

(below) Homes on Mykonos come right up to and sometimes hang over the water surrounding the island.

For centuries, the Greeks have valued education. During the 400 years that Greece was ruled by the Turks, schools were seen as one of the most important ways of keeping Greek culture alive. When Greece became independent after the revolt against Turkish rule, elementary school for all children became the law.

Basketball is a popular sport for youth. The Greece Basketball Association runs basketball leagues for students. Greece also has a national team and a league with city teams.

Elementary and high school

Children start school when they are six. In state schools, education is free. Some children go to private schools, especially if their parents want them to learn foreign languages. After six years of grade school, children go to the gymnasium, or high school. These schools specialize in different subjects. Some focus on Greek history, language, culture, and literature. Others specialize in science, while some are vocational schools, teaching commercial or technical skills.

Universities

The universities of Athens and Thessaloniki are the oldest and most important ones in the country. Students must write a university entrance examination, and competition to get into university is stiff. Many students travel abroad for university.

A typical school day

The school bus picks up children around 8 a.m. In places where there is no school bus, public buses run before and after classes so that children can catch one passing close to their school. Students are expected to study hard and respect their teachers. During a short break, which is more like a recess than lunch, children have a snack and play outside until classes begin again. Younger students get home by 2 p.m., while older ones stay until 3:30 p.m. Many parents worry that Greek schools do not teach as many subjects as other European schools.

Even though it is very expensive, families often send their children to private school after regular classes end for the day.

Having fun in school

School is not only a time for studying and books. Greek children enjoy sports such as basketball, volleyball, and soccer. Students put on plays and concerts for their school mates and parents. Making holiday decorations, especially painted Easter eggs, is a favorite arts activity. A trip to the museum, the children's theater, or the site of ancient ruins is almost as good as a holiday.

School break by the seashore! Summer holidays are a time for relaxing and having fun. Summer breaks are between one and two months long, and during the year, school is often closed for religious one-day holidays.

Because during much of the year it so hot in the middle of the day, Greeks start work early. In the afternoon, they take a break and go home for a rest. It is considered impolite to call on someone during nap time.

Many Greeks make their living from the sea, either by fishing or taking tourists out on trips.

Open for business

For most shops and businesses, the day begins at 8 a.m. and ends around 2 p.m.— on Monday, Wednesday, and Saturday, that is. On Tuesday, Thursday, and Friday, most businesses shut down at 1:30 p.m. and reopen at 5 p.m. They close for the day at about 8:30 p.m. Companies that do business with other countries keep a 9 a.m. to 5 p.m. workday.

Being boss

Most Greeks prefer to own and run their own business. Instead of going to big supermarkets, they buy their groceries from someone they know. Villages, towns, and even big cities have family-owned butcher shops, bakeries, and grocery stores. In every neighborhood, there are many small shops and *períptera*, tiny booths that sell all sorts of products, from magazines, candy and soft drinks, to wrist watches, stuffed toys, and sunglasses.

Family affair

In family-owned businesses, every member of the family chips in and helps. Parents and grandparents take turns looking after the shop. In cafés and restaurants, father may cook, and mother and children serve the customers. When they are not in school, it is not unusual to see children aged nine or ten waiting tables or clearing dishes. If children are too young to carry plates, they sweep the floor or wipe the tables. Everyone helps wash the dishes.

*(below) A sidewalk **períptera** offers a variety of snacks, soft drinks, and other products.*

(above) A street vendor in the middle of a busy market.

Coffee time!

Greeks love coffee, but it is unusual to see a coffeepot in an office. Greeks prefer to order out. Waiters or shopkeepers in white aprons carry trays of *ellinikó kafé*, a very strong coffee topped with frothy, steamed milk, through the streets to neighboring offices.

Greek cities are busy places, filled with people, noise, high-rise buildings, and traffic. Office workers rush to their jobs, groups of children wait for school buses on the street corners, and traffic police try to keep cars moving. Everyone seems to be in a hurry.

Importing trends

Xenomania is a Greek word meaning the love of things that are foreign. Nowhere in Greece is that love more obvious than in the cities. Everyday life for many urban Greeks is filled with items from all over the world. People standing on street corners or riding on buses talk on cellular phones. The streets are crowded with foreign cars, and the shops are filled with **imported** goods of every kind. People wear clothing designed in Paris or New York. Jeans, T-shirts, and running shoes are popular among the young. Many visitors to the cities from the islands or the countryside say they feel nervous asking for directions. They can no longer tell a Greek from a foreigner!

Even in Athens, Greece's biggest, and busiest city, everyday life has its quiet moments. In the Pláka district, a homeowner fixes a light on his house.

22

A sea of concrete

Greek cities are growing so quickly that they can hardly keep up with the thousands of people moving into them each year. In some sections, block after block of six-story concrete apartment buildings are home to many families. Often, the residents are related to each other — aunts, uncles, cousins, and grandparents all living in the same building.

A typical day

Morning starts in a rush. The children are getting ready to meet the school bus and parents are heading off for work. Greeks are not big breakfast eaters, and family members might have a piece of bread with butter and honey, warm milk, or yogurt. Children take a snack to school, perhaps *spanikopita*, a cheese and spinach pie, or some olives and cheese. Some children have grandmothers waiting to care for them. When they get home in the afternoon, a big lunch is waiting for them.

In the evening, the family gathers together. Parents help the children with their homework, and later, everyone relaxes in front of the television. Greek children have dinner later than North Americans, around 8 p.m., and are put to bed before their parents eat around 10 p.m. On the weekends, the children get to stay up later, and sometimes the family goes out for a meal and a movie.

(above) The ancient past is never too far from the present in Greek cities.

(right) A child feeds ducks in a quiet city park.

Children growing up in the country have fewer of the latest gadgets, such as video games and electronic toys, than city children. On weekends and holidays, country children work in the fields with their parents and learn to take on grownup responsibilities. They spend their free time at the agora, the main square of the village, where families shop, enjoy an ice cream, or chat with their friends.

Life in a mountain village

In many mountain villages, homes are built so close together that they share walls. Houses cluster around a square with a church at the center. Smaller churches and shrines dot the surrounding fields and hills.

Many mountain villagers earn their living by shepherding livestock or tending small farms. Others cultivate orchards of chestnuts, walnuts, peaches, pears, cherries, apples, and olives. In the winter, families earn extra income by knitting sweaters or weaving rugs that are taken to the cities and sold to tourists.

Living on the plains

For centuries, people have farmed the flat plains, the most fertile lands of Greece. They are hot and humid in the summer but muddy and drenched in rain in the winter. Farming families live in villages where the houses are next to each other. Farmers may own their land, rent it from wealthy landowners, or work on someone else's farm. Each morning, both men and women ride donkeys or tractors to the fields.

During the spring, summer, and fall, farmers are busy all day planting, fertilizing their fields, and harvesting their crops. In the winter, life is easier. Men play cards or chat in village cafés. Women have time to visit their friends.

An Orthodox priest hurries across a street with his heavy bags.

Roma life

During the harvest season, traveling Roma people set up roadside tent camps on the plains. They work as day laborers. Life is difficult, and the pay is low. Many Roma earn only enough money to allow them to continue their nomadic way of life. After work each evening, the camp fills with the delicious smell of food cooking on an open fire. Roma children sometimes go to local schools where they learn to speak Greek.

Market gossip

Saturday markets in the country towns give people a chance to meet one another and catch up on the latest local news. Farmers from the countryside set up stalls and sell their goods. Women shop for the freshest produce and haggle for a bargain. Groups of men sip strong coffee in the local cafés. Bearded Orthodox priests, in long black cassocks and tall black hats, mingle with widows dressed in black, and teenagers in jeans and T-shirts.

In some small towns and villages, such as the mainland town of Xainthi, people close off the main square to traffic on Saturday evenings for *nifpazaro*, the bride's fair. This custom originally gave young men a chance to exchange looks with girls of marrying age. Today, it offers the whole community an opportunity to get together.

(above) **For more than half the year, tourists invade the narrow marble streets of some Greek villages.**

(below) **Homes in many farming villages are packed tightly together. Farmers walk out to their fields.**

25

Until recently, people living on the Greek islands were very isolated from the mainland. On some islands, the occasional boat bringing supplies and food was the only contact with the outside world. Many islanders were very poor, supporting their families by fishing and raising sheep and goats. Many people left, seeking a better life on the mainland or in other countries. Today, life has changed. Regular boat service and car ferries bring tourists all summer long.

Busy summers

During the hot summer months, Greeks from the mainland and tourists from other countries flock to the islands. They come to sunbathe on the sandy beaches, swim in the crystal clear sea, buy souvenirs, and enjoy the warm hospitality of their island hosts. During these months, the shops, hotels, taxis, cafés, and tavernas are very busy, and islanders work long hours. Most businesses are family-owned, and parents expect their children to help.

(above) The whitewashed building and blue doors are typical of many island homes.

(below) Donkeys are an efficient form of transportation on narrow, hilly island streets.

Lonely in the winter

In the winter, when squalls hit, the islands practically shut down. During bad storms, the sea is so rough that boats bringing food and supplies may not sail for days, even weeks. Most islands do not have hospitals, and when the boats cannot sail, helicopters fly people out in an emergency. People can feel very isolated, although after the busy summer, they are happy for a rest.

The harbor of Skopelos, in the Sporades islands, is a jumble of white houses and small churches against a green landscape.

Looking away from the sea

The sea, which has traditionally provided a living for islanders, suffers from overfishing. Fish are now caught far out at sea. Much of the fish that is served in Greek restaurants is imported from other countries and is actually cheaper than locally caught, fresh fish.

Dynamite: a tribute to the dead

When the sea claims the life of a fisherman or sponge-diver from the island of Kalymnos, a stick of dynamite is hurled into the sea from the top of a cliff. The explosion announces the death and honors the tragic loss.

For thousands of years, Greeks have believed in the importance of exercise and sport. The ancient Greeks built gymnasiums and stadiums where men and boys trained every day. Some ancient sporting events, such as track, gymnastics, and discus and javelin throwing, are still popular.

Really rough

Some sports played in ancient Greece, such as wrestling and boxing, were much rougher than today's versions. Contestants were often badly hurt in a game called *pankration*, which combined wrestling with boxing and kicking. Biting and eye poking were all part of the game. The fight lasted until one opponent showed that he had been defeated by raising a finger — if he still had the strength. Some players even died.

Greece is surrounded by water. The sea and wind make water sports such as parasailing, windsurfing, sailing, and diving popular.

(above) Modern marathon runners compete on a trail near Mount Olympus.

(below) An ancient Minoan fresco depicts boys boxing. Fitness was important to the ancient Greeks.

Modern Greek games and sports

Soccer, which the Greeks call football, is the most popular sport in Greece today. Professional soccer matches take place almost every Sunday afternoon during the season. Basketball is also very popular and Greek teams compete in the country and in the rest of Europe. A favorite pastime for fans, even in remote villages, is to gather at the local café and watch national and international basketball games on television.

In Athens, there are horse races every Monday, Wednesday, and Saturday. Water sports are very popular among Greeks. Windsurfing and parasailing are growing in popularity. Swimming in the warm waters of Greece's many beaches is another favorite activity.

Toys and pastimes

If Greek children made a list of their favorite toys, games, and pastimes, it would not be all that different from a list of things that European and North American kids like. Greek children watch television, go to the latest movie, and play sports such as soccer, basketball, and volleyball. In all but the most remote regions, DVD and computer games are probably the most popular pastimes for Greek children today.

Komboloi

Throughout Greece, people can sometimes be seen fingering a string of beads made of wood, amber, or plastic. Greeks find that handling these beads, called *komboloi*, or sometimes *komposkini*, calms and relaxes them. The *komboloi* acts as an instrument for meditation, and an **amulet**.

Challenges for the future

Over the last century, Greece has changed from a depressed, war-torn country, to a prosperous, modern nation. As Greeks look to the future, they know they will have to deal with the problems and challenges of growth.

Leaving the farm

Many Greeks have moved into the cities over the past 50 years. This has meant that fewer young people are working on farms or in small, family-run businesses. In the cities, especially Athens, services such as education, housing, and transportation need to be improved. Many wealthier Greeks are building country homes on land that used to be forests. Often, the land is cleared through acts of **arson**, which endanger lives and destroy wildlife habitat. The increasing numbers of tourists take a toll on the environment as well. In dry areas, more water is used to provide tourists with the daily showers and luxuries they expect. More garbage is created and must be disposed.

Facing the challenge

Greece is trying to find ways to deal with these problems. Highways and railroads are being extended into remote areas to connect them to the rest of the country. Greeks are trying to find ways of creating a healthier environment. To decrease air pollution, a major problem in Athens, people are allowed to drive only on certain days of the week, depending on whether their cars have odd or even-numbered license plates. Tourist operations are moving to more eco-friendly practices. The government is even cracking down on developers who build houses on land cleared through arson fire.

(right) Donkeys have much less of an impact on the environment than cars, and they are a necessity in some remote Greek villages.

(below) Because Athens is often choked with air pollution, some downtown streets are closed to traffic on certain days of the week.

Glossary

amulet An object worn or used to protect and bring good luck

arson Fires that are deliberately set

city-state An independent state in ancient Greece that ruled over its surrounding territory much like a country

civilization An advanced state of society where there is much culture, government, and science.

descrimination Ill treatment of someone based on their race, class, sex, or religion

feminist movement The women's movement that works for equality for women in the job market, wages, education, and politics

foreign Coming from another country

Greek Orthodox The Eastern Orthodox Christian church that most Greeks belong to

homogeneous Of the same or similar nature

immigrant A person who settles in another country

import To bring goods into a country from another country

impoverish To make poor

nannies People who are paid to look after children

Nazi The group of Germans and others who joined them and followed a brutal program of control and violence throughout Europe during World War II

persecute To treat in a way that causes suffering, especially because of religious beliefs

World War II An international war, fought from 1939-1945 between the Allies (Great Britain, Canada, Australia, the United States, the USSR, Greece, and many other countries) and the Axis (Germany, Japan, Italy, and many other countries)

 # Index